WHEN SLEEPING BIRDS FLY:
365 Amazing Facts About The Animal Kingdom

Sally Meadows

PRAISE FOR
When Sleeping Birds Fly:
365 AMAZING FACTS ABOUT THE ANIMAL KINGDOM

"I dare you to read this remarkable collection of animal facts without a gasp, a chuckle, raised eyebrows, or a nod of affirmation. Sally Meadows' impressive research has unearthed a fascinating menu of details to tease your appetite whether consumed in one-a-day nibbles or irresistible gulps. It's a treat for every nature lover."

– Gillian Richardson,
award-winning author of
10 Plants That Shook The World
and *10 Routes That Crossed the World*

"*When Sleeping Birds Fly* is full of fun facts that make us rethink our understanding of the animal world and reflect on our own place in nature's cycle. From birds cleaning crocodile teeth to octopuses decorating their home with seashells, we learn about animals' amazing inventions, warm compassion, musical talents, and architectural skills to name just a few. An amazing read for all ages."

– Miriam Körner,
children's book author

"Sally Meadows has written a charming and informative book filled with delightful and fascinating tidbits about the natural world. Reading this will persuade you to look up and out at the surprising beauty all around us."

– Alice Kuipers, author of
Polly Diamond and the Magic Book

"*When Sleeping Birds Fly* offers a fresh presentation of the kinds of bite-sized wonderments that information–hungry kids (and their grown-ups!) love. Sally has organized amazing and true animal trivia by themes that spark a sense of personal connection and empathy toward our living world."

– Dr. Sandy Bonny,
writer, artist, & science educator

"In her latest book, *When Sleeping Birds Fly*, Sally Meadows both shocks and delights readers with her clever grouping of amazing facts about the animal kingdom. What fun to read through the many fabulous, fascinating facts about familiar and not so familiar creatures. From poop ammunition to crocodiles climbing trees, there is nothing dull about *When Sleeping Birds Fly*. Read it in its entirety, or enjoy it one category at a time."

**– Glynis M Belec,
award-winning children's author,
freelance writer, & inspirational speaker**

"Prepare to be amazed at these bite-sized fun facts about creatures near and far. This book will whet your curiosity and quite possibly make you laugh out loud."

**– Sharon Plumb,
author of *Draco's Child***

"Whether or not you are an animal lover, and no matter your age, you will learn something new that excites or surprises you in Sally's book. It is a reminder of how big, beautiful, and wondrous the world, and animal kingdom, truly is."

**– Darla Read,
postpartum doula and parent**

"*When Sleeping Birds Fly* is a delightful and captivating book chock full of amazing and quirky facts about animals, birds, fish, and bugs. Sally Meadows has gathered wonderfully entertaining information and given it to the reader in delectable bite-sized pieces. Reading it made me want to look up the creatures she talks of and continue learning more about them. This is a book that is sure to inspire awe in children and adults alike."

**– Wendy Crawford,
retired teacher**

WHEN SLEEPING BIRDS FLY:
365 Amazing Facts About The Animal Kingdom

Sally Meadows

Copyright © 2018 by Sally Meadows
https://sallymeadows.com

All rights reserved. No part of this book may be reproduced or transmitted in any form or by any means, electronic or mechanical, including photocopying, recording, or by any information storage and retrieval system, without permission in writing from the publisher.

ISBN: 978-1-988983-02-8

Published by Siretona Creative, Calgary, AB
www.siretona.com

Cover Design: Ellen Hooge
Interior Design: Colleen McCubbin and Ellen Hooge

PHOTO AND CLIPART CREDITS
https://openclipart.org

COVERS
Photo licence: Creative Commons Attribution 2.0 Generic (CC BY 2.0)
- Front cover: Frigate Bird/Jeff Hart/17-03-2010
- Back cover: frigate bird following the ship/Ollie Harridge/15-05-2008

SECTION HEADERS
Open Clipart licence: Creative Commons Zero 1.0 Public Domain License
- Wooden sign-post/Bonzo/07-17-2014
- Message in a bottle/TomK 32/04-15-2017
- Mirror – lineart/frankes/06-04-2015
- Casa-house/migranerp/01-25-2014
- Light bulb/Firkin/09-07-2016
- Funny music note/anonymous/02-05-16
- Comedy and Tragedy masks/J4p4n/06-23-2017
- Chick from egg/mcol/09-16-07
- Baby bottle (outlines)/m1981/08-09-2015
- Place setting/Firkin/10-22-2017
- Starry night: star/nicubunu/03-31-2013
- Happy tooth/tawm1972/02-22-2012
- Salivating smiley face/GDJ/03-12-2016
- Kawaii toilet/J4p4n/05-21-2017
- Magic rabbit/bogdan/08-25-16
- Funny glasses/ghosthand/09-20-2011
- Skull and crossbones/ryan erch/12-26-2006
- Treasure chest/oksmith/03-15-2018
- Gold medal award/Juhele/12-21-2017
- Toilet paper - the end is near/doodleguy/09-12-2013

CONTENTS

Introduction	9
From Here To There	11
Helping Others	15
Just Like Us	17
Home, Sweet Home	21
Innovation and Intelligence	26
Music, Sweet Music	30
Communication and Emotions	33
Dating and Mating	37
Pregnancy and Birth	45
Babies	51
Meal Time	55
Nighty-Night	59
Body Parts	61
Amazing Senses	73
Poop, Pee, and Gas Tales	76
Sneaky Tricks	82
When Danger Threatens	85
Disguises	94
Deadly!	98
Tiny Treasures	103
Humungous!	105
Olympic Worthy	108
When It's Cold Out	110
Odds and Ends	112
Questions	120
Answers	123
Author's Note	124
About the Author	125
Also by the Author	127
Coming Soon	127

INTRODUCTION

This world is an endless source of inspiration and wonder! I have spent hundreds of hours poring over a wide variety of materials to find the most astonishing facts I could about the animal kingdom. I hope what you learn in this book delights, enlightens, and inspires you as much as it did me.

I encourage you to use these fun facts as a jumping off point to do your own research on the amazing animal kingdom. You can download FREE extension activity worksheets for *When Sleeping Birds Fly: 365 Amazing Facts About the Animal Kingdom* at: https://sallymeadows.com/free-stuff.

Keep up to date with all my latest news by signing up for my newsletter at: https://sallymeadows.com/.

Sally Meadows

FROM HERE TO THERE

1. When baby shrews go for a walk, they form a "train" by holding onto the tail of the sibling in front with their teeth.

2. Bulldog ants can leap from the ground onto the back of low-flying bees.

3. When a mother-of-pearl caterpillar encounters a predator, it anchors its end to the ground, coils into a circle, and rolls away like a tire.

FROM HERE TO THERE

 The American water shrew can run across the surface of a small pond thanks to air bubbles that get trapped in the fringe of stiff hairs on its feet.

 Crocodiles can climb trees.

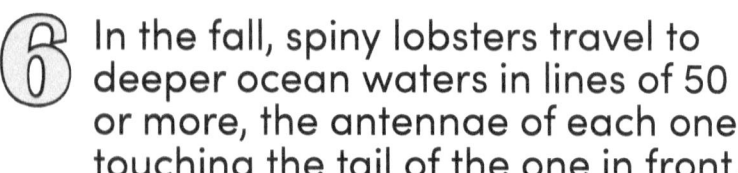 In the fall, spiny lobsters travel to deeper ocean waters in lines of 50 or more, the antennae of each one touching the tail of the one in front.

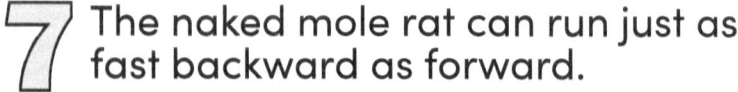 The naked mole rat can run just as fast backward as forward.

FROM HERE TO THERE

⑧ Tiger beetles run so fast they can temporarily blind themselves.

⑨ Every day hundreds of thousands of golden jellyfish swim from one end of Jellyfish Lake (on the island of Palau in the Pacific Ocean) to the other end and back again, following the path of the sun. The jellyfish have tiny algae living in them that need the energy of the sun to survive.

⑩ The young smooth fan lobster hitches a ride on a moon jellyfish and eats its host as they travel around together.

FROM HERE TO THERE

11 The Atlantic bluefin tuna pulls its fins into slots on its body to increase its sleekness so it can move faster through the water.

12 A baby broad-snouted caiman (a reptile that resembles an alligator) rides in its mother's mouth.

13 Polar bears are strong swimmers but they prefer to get around by using chunks of ice as rafts.

14 Snails sometimes travel in the slime tracks of other snails to save energy.

HELPING OTHERS

15 When a sperm whale is injured, members of its pod circle around it and support it at the water's surface.

16 Rove beetles cling to the fur around the neck of Central American mice and rats when they are out and about. When the rodents return to their burrows, the beetles jump off and rid the nest of fleas.

HELPING OTHERS

17 Coral reefs have areas where cleaner shrimps service fish. The fish open their gills and mouths to show that they want help, and the cleaners remove lice, trim off loose skin, and remove fungal growth.

18 Humpback whales have been known to defend sea lions, grey whale calves, and seals from orcas—even though orcas are one of their own deadliest enemies.

19 Ugandan mongooses climb up on the backs of warthogs and eat the ticks that annoy their host.

20 An Egyptian plover (bird) perches in a crocodile's open mouth and cleans its teeth without fear of being eaten.

21 Koalas have fingerprints that look like those of humans.

22 African chimpanzees hug, kiss, laugh, play-wrestle, and tickle each other.

23 Japanese macaques (snow monkeys) enjoy taking dips in hot springs and throwing snowballs at each other.

JUST LIKE US

24 Ants can tell the difference between sweet, sour, salty, and bitter flavours.

25 The South American freshwater pacu fish has teeth that look almost exactly like human teeth.

26 The demosponge removes unwanted materials from its body by contracting and forcing water out along with whatever was irritating it—similar to how we sneeze.

27 Parrots high-five each other...with their feet.

JUST LIKE US

28 Ants care for and protect aphids, similar to how farmers tend to their livestock. Aphids feed on the dew of plants and ooze out sugar-rich honeydew, which ants love. Some ants will "milk" the aphids for honeydew by stroking their abdomens with their antennae.

29 Mice show facial expressions such as fear, hunger, and hurt.

30 Young goats have baby teeth that they lose when their adult teeth come in.

31 Ants look at several possibilities for a home before picking the one that best fits their needs.

JUST LIKE US

32 Cats are either right pawed or left pawed.

33 Crows play pranks on each other.

34 Male kangaroos flex their biceps to impress females.

HOME SWEET HOME

35 The Asian tailorbird uses its beak to poke holes along the edges of a large leaf. It then laces the leaf edges together with spider silk or plant fiber to form a cradle within which it builds its cozy nest.

36 A badger makes its home in easy-to-dig sandy soil, creating separate spaces for a bathroom, sleeping, and a nursery.

37 The male starling weaves fresh herbs into its nest to help boost the immune system of its babies.

HOME, SWEET HOME

38 Some octopuses decorate their dens with shells, rocks, and shiny objects.

39 A meerkat's burrow has about 70 escape routes.

40 Himalayan honeybees build their nests under rock ledges on the faces of high-altitude vertical cliffs.

41 Army ants cling to each other to form a living, ball-shaped nest. The inside of the nest includes passages, as well as separate chambers for the queen, eggs, larvae, and food.

HOME, SWEET HOME

42 The female hummingbird uses spider silk to glue together her tiny nest of grass, leaves, flower petals, and other materials. The fuzzy parts of cattails or dandelions line the nest, and moss or lichen is put on the outside wall for camouflage.

43 The sea cucumber, which breathes through its rear end, provides a daytime home for the eel-like pearlfish. The pearlfish waits for the sea cucumber to take a breath then swims inside.

44 The nest of one kind of spider wasp contains an outer chamber made up of dead ants to scare off predators.

HOME, SWEET HOME

45 The sociable weavers of South Africa and southern Namibia create one huge tree nest for hundreds of birds. Inside are chambers, one for each bird family, lined with soft materials such as fur, fluff, and cotton.

46 Some cave-dwelling swiftlets build their nests entirely from threads of their own saliva.

47 Weaver ants create a nest by squeezing a silky thread out of one of their larvae, attaching one end of the thread to a leaf, carrying the larva to another leaf close by, attaching the thread there, and repeating back and forth until they have woven their home.

HOME, SWEET HOME

48 The dusky scrubfowl's nest, made of twigs and decomposing leaves, can measure more than 11 m (36 ft) in diameter and 5 m (16 ft) high.

49 One species of the mason bee makes its nest from flower petals cemented together by nectar and mud. Iranian mason bees use only purple flowers.

INNOVATION AND INTELLIGENCE

50 The caterpillar of the case-bearing clothes moth knits its own wooly, protective "sweater" from the garment it destroys.

51 The sunburst diving beetle carries an air bubble with it when it dives underwater so it can breathe.

52 The brown-headed nuthatch holds a small piece of bark in its bill and pries up other pieces of bark on a tree to get at insects and eggs hidden underneath.

INNOVATION AND INTELLIGENCE

53 Wasps are experts at geometry, using their antennae as rulers and protractors to form perfectly shaped hexagon cells for their nests.

54 New Caledonian crows shape sticks into hooks and spears then poke them into tree crevices to retrieve larvae and insects.

55 Female bottlenose dolphins hold sea sponges in their mouths as they dig up the sandy seafloor to reveal hidden prey. Scientists believe that the sponge acts as a shovel, protective mask, or both.

INNOVATION AND INTELLIGENCE

56 Bats, mice, and squirrels that live in the city have bigger brains—which suggests they are smarter—than their country counterparts.

57 The weaverbird uses its beak and feet to tie knots in the vegetation pieces it uses to build its nest, making it more secure.

58 Monkeys use twigs, hair, feathers, grass, and/or coconut fiber to floss their teeth.

59 Worker ants form a bridge with their bodies when they need to reach higher branches of a tree for food.

INNOVATION AND INTELLIGENCE

60 After an adult brine fly emerges from its underwater pupal casing, it surrounds itself with an air bubble and floats to the surface to begin its new life in the air.

61 Female beavers do most of the planning and engineering work when building a lodge. The male's role is to inspect the structure and patch leaks.

62 Chimpanzees, tamarins, and gorillas know what plants to eat to counteract the effects of illnesses and parasites.

63 In the fall, chickadees grow extra brain cells to help them remember where they have hidden seeds.

MUSIC SWEET MUSIC

64 Male and female siamang gibbon pairs sing together to strengthen their bond. They sing more when they first pair than when they have been together for a while.

65 The humpback whale's beautiful mating song can last an hour or longer.

66 Male northern mockingbirds learn up to 200 different songs during their lifetime. They also sing more when there is a full moon.

MUSIC, SWEET MUSIC

67 Mosquitoes typically buzz in the key of D. The common housefly buzzes in the key of F.

68 A female zebra finch chooses the male that sings the longest or most complex song as the best mate to provide for her young.

69 The North American brown thrasher can sing more than 2000 different songs.

70 The superb lyrebird of Australia not only mimics other birds' songs, it also imitates other sounds it has heard such as chainsaws and camera clicks.

MUSIC, SWEET MUSIC

71 A whale has a range of at least seven octaves yet has no vocal chords.

72 When you slow down the notes of the woodlark's song, they show a structure similar to Bach's preludes and fugues. The skylark's song resembles parts of Beethoven's 5th symphony.

73 A canary can sing two different songs at the same time.

74 The yellow-headed blackbird's love song ends in a bray that sounds like a dying donkey.

COMMUNICATION AND EMOTIONS

75 Geckos communicate by barking, chirping, and squeaking.

76 Most dogs have about 100 different facial expressions. However, some breeds such as pit bulls have only a tenth of those. These dogs often get into fights because other dogs misread them.

77 Japanese macaques have different vocal accents depending on where they live.

COMMUNICATION AND EMOTIONS

78 White-faced capuchin monkeys greet each other by sticking their fingers up each other's noses.

79 Asiatic golden cats in the south of China sometimes communicate by spitting.

80 When an elephant dies, the other elephants cover the body up with ripped-up grass, leaves, and/or tree branches. Even many years after a death, the elephants may visit the place their loved one died and caress the bones with their trunks.

81 White lady spiders of the Namib Desert in Africa tap on the sand to send messages to other spiders.

COMMUNICATION AND EMOTIONS

82 Dolphins can make over 2000 different sounds, including whistles, clicks, and barks. They also communicate through touching fins.

83 Black-tailed prairie dogs greet each other by gently touching teeth. To us, it looks like they're kissing.

84 The beluga uses different facial expressions to get its message across in addition to its trills, clicks, moos, and squeaks.

85 Baby Nile crocodiles call out to their siblings and mother when it's time to hatch.

COMMUNICATION AND EMOTIONS

86 When a common green magpie discovers another magpie has died, it calls out loudly to attract others. Up to 40 magpies noisily gather around the body for about 10-15 minutes then fly off without a sound.

87 An octopus changes colour to camouflage itself, scare away rivals, and to express its emotions such as interest in a potential mate.

88 The common crane has a reddish patch of bare skin on its head that becomes bright red when it gets excited or angry.

89 One species of cichlid (a fish) pees to communicate.

DATING AND MATING

90 To attract a mate, the male satin bowerbird creates a home made of sticks (called a bower) and paints the walls with his bill after dipping it into chewed-up berries. He decorates his home with brightly coloured natural and found objects, most often blue in colour. He may also hold something blue in his beak to highlight his blue colouring. When a female arrives, he struts and bows, opens his wings and shakes, and makes rattling or buzzing noises.

DATING AND MATING

91 To attract a female, the male great crested newt does a handstand and waves his tail in front of her.

92 If the male redback spider doesn't complete an elaborate, 100-minute long dance to impress her, the female kills him.

93 Seahorses dance with each other every day during the mating period. They often twist tails together and change colour as they move.

94 During courtship, sandhill cranes hop, bow, twirl, flap their wings, coo, and leap into the air.

DATING AND MATING

95 During courting season, bald eagles lock talons in the air and whirl around each other in tight circles, falling in a "death spiral" and letting go before they hit the ground.

96 Swans mate for life. When two swans touch beaks together to "kiss," their necks form a heart.

97 A male chameleon turns a bright colour to attract a female. A female turns a bright colour to reject a male.

98 The female Arctic tern will not mate until the male brings her a gift of food.

DATING AND MATING

99 A male ostracod is a tiny sea creature that tries to attract a mate with a trail of blue puffs of light—chemicals that shoot out of his body as he swims.

100 The male shell-brooding cichlid uses his impressive shell collection to attract females. His mate will lay her eggs in her favourite shell from his collection.

101 A male orchid bee travels long distances to collect a variety of scents, which he stores in special chambers in his hind legs. When he spots a female, he spreads the scents on his wings and flutters around her.

DATING AND MATING

102 The love call of male cicadas can be as loud as a chainsaw—up to 120 decibels.

103 The male Wilson's bird-of-paradise attracts a female by clearing an area of the forest floor and using it as a stage for his calls, struts, dances, and flips.

104 A male scorpion tries to impress a female by spreading his claws to make them look bigger. The two then lock claws and dance for hours before mating.

105 A female western meadowlark prefers a brightly coloured male, as he controls the best territory.

DATING AND MATING

106 The tiny, 5 mm (0.2 in) long peacock spider lifts and waves his colourful stomach flap like a fan during his courtship dance. He jumps, struts, and sways to attract the female, who watches the male intently before deciding if she wants him as a partner.

107 The female tarantula sometimes eats the male after mating if she's hungry and he doesn't leave fast enough.

108 Male emperor moths can detect the perfume given off by mate-seeking females up to 11 km (7 mi) away.

DATING AND MATING

109 Every year between October and December millions of red crabs that live in the forest of Christmas Island (in the Indian Ocean) emerge at exactly the same time to journey down to the sea to mate.

110 To attract attention during mating season, the male great frigatebird puffs out his bright red throat pouch to form a balloon-like "valentine." If the female frigatebird likes what she sees, she rests her head on his "love cushion."

111 The faces of both male and female Japanese macaques turn bright red during the mating season.

DATING AND MATING

112 A male betta fish opens its gills, spreads its fins, and does a dance if interested in a female. The female will respond by darkening in colour, and vertical lines will appear on her body.

113 When mating, the male anglerfish grabs onto the much larger female with his mouth, hangs on, and gradually fuses with her body. All his body parts disintegrate except for what's needed to fertilize her eggs.

PREGNANCY AND BIRTH

114 The female seahorse lays her eggs inside a special pouch found on the male's body. He fertilizes the eggs, takes care of them, and gives birth to the babies.

115 Some female manta rays give birth while leaping out of the water.

116 The male jawfish holds hundreds of his mate's eggs in his open mouth for the five to seven days it takes to hatch them. He will not eat during this period of time.

PREGNANCY AND BIRTH

117 The black-spotted sticky frog female lays her eggs in the deadly pitcher plant, which kills and digests most insects and small animals that fall into it. Her eggs and tadpoles are miraculously immune.

118 The common frilled shark has the longest pregnancy of any animal—42 months (3.5 years).

119 When temperatures are hot (above 33°C, 91°F), alligator babies are born male. When temperatures are cool (below 30°C, 86°F), only female babies hatch. When birthed between these temperatures, there is a roughly even mix of male and female.

PREGNANCY AND BIRTH

120 To keep its one egg at the right temperature, a northern gannet (bird) stands on top of it.

121 The female giant water bug lays eggs on her mate's back and glues them down so he doesn't lose them.

122 Female mountain goats give birth on steep cliffs.

123 The common tenrec, a mammal native to Madagascar, gives birth to as many as 32 babies at once.

PREGNANCY AND BIRTH

124 Baby Suriname toads are born from "pockets" under the skin on their mother's back.

125 When his offspring are born, the male Siberian dwarf hamster licks them clean, cuts the umbilical cord with his teeth, and takes care of the newborns.

126 The common green lacewing makes dozens of thin silky stalks, attaching one end of each to a leaf. She then places an egg at the free end of the stalk so it is out of reach of predators such as ants.

PREGNANCY AND BIRTH

127 Lemmings can have babies when they are only one month old.

128 When the male túngara frog finds a mate, the female carries him to a special spot she has chosen for her nursery. She squirts out a mess of eggs and jelly, which the male whips into a foamy mass with his back feet. The eggs hatch after a few days.

129 The female paper nautilus protects her eggs by oozing goo from the tips of two of her tentacles and creating a structure that hardens into a fancy shell. She places the eggs inside and climbs in too.

PREGNANCY AND BIRTH

130 The female gastric brooding frog of Australia swallows her eggs so she can hatch them in her stomach. The jelly surrounding the eggs stops the stomach from producing acid. After the eggs hatch, the tadpoles take about six to eight weeks to develop. When the time is right, they crawl up out of her mouth. The mother is unable to eat during this time.

BABIES

131 A newborn koala is about the size of a jellybean.

132 When an elephant baby feels safe and secure, it makes a purring noise.

133 Baby seahorses float in small groups and use their tails to cling to each other.

BABIES

134 The male American finfoot carries his chicks in special pouches under his wings, even when flying.

135 All female baboons in a troop help take care of the babies.

136 Dolphin babies are born tail first.

137 Loon and grebe young ride on their parents' backs. They learn to swim when a parent suddenly dives, leaving the babies bobbing in the water. The parents resurface a short distance away so that the chicks must swim to them.

BABIES

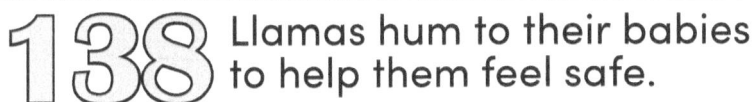 Llamas hum to their babies to help them feel safe.

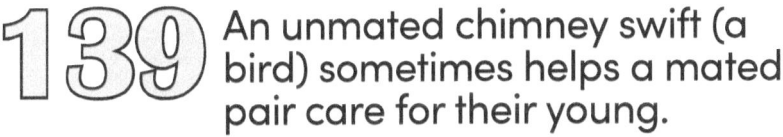 An unmated chimney swift (a bird) sometimes helps a mated pair care for their young.

140 Mother whales caress their babies with their fins.

141 Some types of mouse opossums have newborns as small as a grain of rice.

BABIES

142 Female kangaroos can have three joeys (babies) at different stages at the same time: one in the womb, one in her pouch, and one out of the pouch being weaned. The growth of the baby in the womb will pause until the one in the pouch is ready to leave.

143 Baby wolf spiders ride on their mother's back.

144 Harpy eagle parents kick their chicks out of the nest if they refuse to leave once they're grown.

145 Fer-de-lance snake young are deadly poisonous right from birth.

146 To get the minerals they need to survive, some butterflies drink turtle tears.

147 Japanese macaques season their food by dipping it in seawater.

148 The lips of giant clams contain algae gardens that produce the sugar and proteins that the clams need to thrive.

MEAL TIME

149 Horned and pied-billed grebes eat their own feathers and also feed them to their young. The feathers protect a grebe's stomach from sharp fish bones and help slow the digestive process so that the bones dissolve before passing into the intestine.

150 A crown-of-thorns starfish feeds by forcing its stomach out through its mouth, stretching it over coral, and digesting nutrients with its stomach juices.

151 A hummingbird drinks the nectar of hundreds of flowers every day. If a hummingbird gets trapped indoors, it will starve to death within an hour.

MEAL TIME

152 The energy spiders get from eating their own webs is used to create more webs.

153 When humpback whales are hungry, they swim in circles below a school of fish, blowing a steady stream of bubbles out of their blowholes and herding the fish into the bubble "net." The whales then take turns swimming through the herded fish with their mouths open.

154 Some baby spiders eat their mother.

155 Flamingos are born pale grey. Their diet of brine shrimp and algae gradually turns their feathers pink.

MEAL TIME

156 The noises Tasmanian devils make when they eat can be heard up to 2 km (1.2 mi) away.

157 When cattle egrets are hungry, they divide their flock into two groups. The first group leapfrogs over the second group, stirring up insects when they land. The insects fly up and are caught by the second group, who then leapfrog over the first group so they can eat too. They repeat this pattern until all have their fill.

158 The tongue-eating isopod is a parasite that eats a fish's tongue. It then becomes the new tongue, feeding on the food the fish catches.

NIGHTY-NIGHT

159 To avoid floating away while napping, sea otters wrap kelp—which grows from the sea floor all the way to the water's surface and acts like an anchor—around themselves.

160 Sperm whales sleep in groups, floating vertically in the water.

161 Great frigatebirds, which can spend days in the air at a time, are able to sleep while flying.

NIGHTY-NIGHT

162 When a Bleeker's parrotfish is ready to sleep, mucus from glands on its body oozes out to form a protective "sleeping bag" that allows it to rest undisturbed by enemies.

163 A dolphin sleeps with half its brain awake so that it can surface to breathe, and be alert for predators.

164 The wrinkle-faced bat pulls up a flap of skin that acts as a mask over its face when it is ready to sleep.

165 Orca mothers go without sleep for a full month after a calf is born.

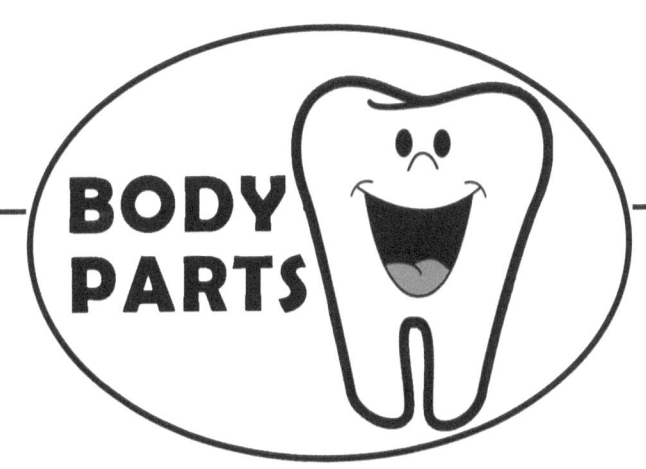

BODY PARTS

166 A trap-jaw ant can snap its jaws together as fast as 230 km/h (143 mph).

167 A hippo's lips are about 0.6 m (2 ft) wide.

168 The pupils of goats' eyes are rectangular.

BODY PARTS

169 Pygmy tarsiers have unusually large eyes for the size of their body. If humans had the same proportion of eyes to body, our eyes would be the size of grapefruits.

170 The praying mantis has only one ear, and it's in the centre of its chest.

171 A chameleon's tongue travels 21 km/h (13 mph), fast enough to capture a fly midair.

172 A narwhal has two big teeth in its upper jaws. When a male narwhal becomes an adult, its right tooth stops growing, but its left tooth pushes through its upper lip, growing a tusk up to 3 m (almost 10 ft) in length.

BODY PARTS

173 You can see a glass frog's heart beating through its transparent skin.

174 The klipspringer (African antelope) has tiny pads on its hooves that act as suction cups. These help it balance when walking on rocky terrain.

175 A walking stick (insect) can regrow a lost leg or antenna.

176 A whale's earwax plug can be as long as 25 cm (10 in) and can give information about the whale's life history.

BODY PARTS

177 The peanut-head bug has a hollow dome on its head that looks like an unshelled peanut.

178 The reddish oil in an Arctic tern's eyes acts like built-in sunglasses.

179 A hummingbird's heart is about the size of a cranberry.

180 A lobster's teeth are in its stomach, and its stomach is found behind its eyes.

BODY PARTS

181 A midge (insect) beats its wings more than 62,000 times a minute.

182 The axolotl (aquatic salamander) can regrow lost limbs and self-heal injured body parts.

183 The octopus has nine brains: a central one, and one at the end of each arm.

184 Beavers' teeth grow 10 times faster than human fingernails.

BODY PARTS

185 A snake's eyes are always open.

186 A toucan's tongue looks like a long, skinny feather.

187 Honeybees have hair on their eyes.

188 A beaver has a transparent eyelid that comes down over each eye, and flaps that close its nostrils and ears, while swimming. It also has inner lips behind its front teeth to avoid getting water in its mouth while carrying sticks underwater.

BODY PARTS

189 A water scorpion uses its long tail as a snorkel—by holding the tip above the water's surface—so that it can breathe underwater.

190 When a flatfish is born, it has one eye on each side of its body. As the fish grows, one eye moves around the body until it is on the same side as the other eye.

191 A lobster's blood is colourless. When its blood is exposed to air, the copper in it reacts with oxygen and turns the blood blue.

192 A cockroach can survive for weeks without a head because its brain doesn't control breathing.

BODY PARTS

193 The skin of walruses is up to 10 cm (4 in) thick.

194 The barreleye (fish) has upward-pointing, barrel-shaped eyes that are protected by a transparent, fluid-filled dome.

195 The red-eyed tree frog is neon green with bulging red eyes, orange feet, and bright blue and yellow sides.

196 The okapi, which is related to the giraffe, has stripes like a zebra, ears like a donkey, and a tongue like an anteater.

BODY PARTS

197 Some butterflies' ears are on their wings.

198 A suction cup on the underside of the northern clingfish is so strong that the fish is able to pull mollusks up to 150 times its own weight off the seafloor.

199 The Indian giant squirrel has purple fur.

200 The basking shark's liver, which contains lightweight oil and hydrocarbons to keep it buoyant in water, is almost one quarter its total body weight.

BODY PARTS

201 The praying mantis is the only insect that can look over its shoulder.

202 Severed sea star arms can grow new bodies.

203 Caterpillars have mouths, but butterflies don't.

204 The glasswing butterfly has transparent wings.

BODY PARTS

205 A leafcutter ant's jaws vibrate 1000 times per second as it saws off parts of leaves.

206 A bullfrog's eyes close when it swallows food. The eyes sink down through openings in its skull and help push the food down its throat.

207 Naked mole rats can move their two front teeth separately like chopsticks.

208 Sea otters carry tools and food in extra folds of skin that act like built-in purses, found under their armpits.

BODY PARTS

209 The giant squid's eyes are 25 cm (10") across—the largest of any animal.

210 An aardvark has the body of a giant, hump-backed rat, the head of an anteater, the ears of a bear, the snout of a pig, the tail of a kangaroo, and the claws of a tiger.

211 The Malaysian stalk-eyed fly's eyes occur at the end of skinny stalks that project from its head.

AMAZING SENSES

212 A shark's sense of smell is 10,000 times better than that of a human.

213 A chameleon's eyes can look in two different directions at once.

214 A snail smells with its lips.

215 Sensors on the bottom of a common housefly's feet let it taste whatever it is walking on.

AMAZING SENSES

216 The blade-like snout of the sawfish can detect the movement and heartbeat of prey, even when the prey is buried in sand.

217 The whirligig beetle has compound eyes that allow it, while floating on water, to see both above and below the surface at the same time.

218 A rabbit can see behind it without moving its head.

219 A mother bat returning to a cave from a hunting trip can pick out her baby among millions of bats by its own special squeak and smell.

AMAZING SENSES

220 The skin on the tentacles around the nose of the star-nosed mole is 20 times more sensitive than human fingertips.

221 A catfish has more than 100,000 taste buds—all over its body.

222 Bees can see blue, green, violet, orange, and yellow, but they can't see the colour red.

223 Although whales' ears are two tiny holes in the skin, they can hear sounds from as far away as 1600 km (994 mi).

POOP PEE AND GAS TALES

224 The parrotfish uses its fused front teeth to gnaw raw coral to get at nutritious algae. The coral crumbles inside the fish and is pooped out as white sand that forms those gorgeous beaches humans love.

225 Wombat poop is cube-shaped.

226 Herrings (fish) communicate by passing gas.

POOP, PEE, AND GAS TALES

227 When it feels threatened, the caterpillar of the skipper butterfly shoots poop pellets at enemies up to 1.5 m (5 ft) away.

228 The pee of the leopard gecko comes out in tiny crystals.

229 Ground nesting birds such as penguins and the blue-footed booby protect their eggs from insects by spraying a ring of poop around their nests.

230 A male hippo spins its tail and sprays poop everywhere to impress a female or to mark its territory when another male comes too close.

POOP, PEE, AND GAS TALES

231 Otter poop smells like jasmine tea.

232 One fifth of the methane gas released into the atmosphere is from insect flatulence.

233 Burrowing owls sometimes line their nests with cow poop.

234 Young pandas require a special type of intestinal bacteria to help them digest the plants they eat. They get these bacteria by eating their parents' poop.

POOP, PEE, AND GAS TALES

235 A housefly poops every few minutes.

236 The larva of a golden tortoise beetle uses a "fork" coming out of its rear end to hold a hardened shield made of its own poop over its body to ward off predators. The shield can be flipped up and down as needed.

237 When golden eagle chicks have to go to the bathroom, they face the centre of the nest and back up to poop over its edge. Because they have accidents while still learning, the parents line the nest with vegetation for easy cleanup.

POOP, PEE, AND GAS TALES

238 The Chinese soft-shelled turtle pees from its mouth.

239 The world's most expensive coffee is made from coffee beans that Asian palm civets (a mammal) have eaten and then pooped out.

240 The Bassian thrush (bird) of eastern Australia passes gas to help it catch its prey. The gas startles nearby worms and insects into revealing where they are hiding so that the thrush can gobble them up.

POOP, PEE, AND GAS TALES

241 After a hummingbird has eaten a fly, it takes only 10 minutes for the waste to come out the other end.

242 If their nesting colony is disturbed, young black-crowned night herons will poop and throw up on the intruder.

243 The turkey vulture poops on its legs to help keep it cool when it's hot outside. The poop also helps disinfect their legs from the bacteria they pick up while scavenging for road kill.

SNEAKY TRICKS

244 The California roadrunner gets rid of its enemy, a rattlesnake, by putting cactus spines around the snake while it sleeps. When the snake wakes up and tries to uncoil, the spines prick it no matter which way it turns. The snake gets angry and with nothing else close by, bites itself and dies of its own poison.

SNEAKY TRICKS

245 The female brown-headed cowbird lays her eggs in other birds' nests. The cowbird baby often outcompetes the other babies for food, grows faster and bigger, and pushes its adopted siblings out of their own nest.

246 Mice can fit through a hole no wider than a pencil.

247 When the thread-legged bug pretends to be caught on a spider's web and a spider comes close to eat it, the spider gets eaten instead.

SNEAKY TRICKS

248 Magpie pairs follow a coyote to try to steal its food. One magpie sneaks up behind the coyote and pulls its tail. When the coyote turns toward it, the other magpie steals the food.

249 House wrens poke holes in the eggs of other birds. They also sabotage other birds' nests and endanger hatchlings by filling the nests with sticks.

WHEN DANGER THREATENS

250 When the veined octopus senses danger, it climbs inside a coconut shell half that's been discarded into the ocean by local villagers, and then pulls another one on top.

251 When a sea cucumber is threatened, it ejects its internal organs out of its rear end and escapes while the predator feasts on its guts. It regenerates its body parts within two weeks.

WHEN DANGER THREATENS

252 The peppermint stick insect defends itself against a predator by spraying a milky, peppermint-scented liquid.

253 Boxer crabs carry stinging sea anemones in their claws for protection.

254 New world tarantulas have sharp hairs on their underside. When a predator comes too close, the tarantula kicks out the hairs using its back legs. The hairs fly through the air like arrows at an enemy target.

WHEN DANGER THREATENS

255 Because the black pebble toad is unable to hop or swim, it rolls itself into a ball and bounces away when a predator comes too close.

256 When it senses danger, the elephant hawk moth caterpillar, which has spots that look like eyes, lifts its front end and inflates it to create what looks like a snake's head.

257 An armadillo lizard can escape from danger by biting its tail and forming a spiky circle that rolls away.

WHEN DANGER THREATENS

258 *Stenamma* ants that nest in clay banks have a clay ball ready to roll into their nest's entryway when a predator approaches.

259 When the spotted skunk is threatened, it stamps its front feet, backs away, and throws its rear end over its head in a handstand, ready to release its unpleasant spray.

260 Black-capped chickadees have a complex vocal warning system that gives specific information about the kind of danger near.

261 The nuthatch has learned to decode the warning calls of black-capped chickadees so that they can keep safe too.

WHEN DANGER THREATENS

262 When danger looms, the Pacific hagfish makes huge amounts of slime from glands in its skin, making it so slippery predators cannot grasp it. To get rid of the slime later, the hagfish ties its body into a knot and slides the knot up and down, scraping away the mucus.

263 French Guiana termites guarding their colony will inflate like a balloon and explode when predators approach, splashing them with a sticky, toxic liquid.

264 When danger comes near, the horny toad flattens itself on the ground and stays still. If the predator still approaches, the toad puffs up its body like a spiky balloon. If that doesn't work, it squirts blood from its eyes.

WHEN DANGER THREATENS

265 When the glass lizard is attacked, its tail drops off, breaking into pieces. The pieces wiggle like snakes, distracting the attacker so the lizard can escape.

266 The vinegaroon (an arachnid) squirts a vinegar-smelling, acetic acid mixture from glands at the base of its tail to scare predators away.

267 When a male hooded seal is threatened, it blows out the skin from inside its nose, forming what looks like a big red balloon on its head.

268 The smiley face on the back of the happy face spider scares away predators such as birds.

WHEN DANGER THREATENS

269 The Mount Lyell salamander curls its head under its back legs and rolls like a wheel when it needs to escape from a predator.

270 When the pied-billed grebe senses a threat, it lowers itself in the water like a submarine by emptying its internal air sacs and squeezing out air between its feathers and body. This leaves only its head above the water's surface, like a periscope.

271 When threatened, the bloody-nosed beetle releases a red, foul tasting fluid from its mouth.

WHEN DANGER THREATENS

272 The grouper's swim bladder produces a booming noise that scares away anything that gets too close to it.

273 When threatened, the Brazilian three-banded armadillo snaps its head and tail together to form an almost perfect, armoured ball.

274 The sponge crab cuts a piece of living sponge to fit over itself to deter predators. Not only is it a disguise, the sponge is also toxic to the crab's enemies.

275 If playing dead doesn't work, click beetles scare predators away by catapulting themselves into the air.

WHEN DANGER THREATENS

276 The Iberian ribbed newt pushes its poison-coated, razor sharp ribs through its sides to protect itself against a predator.

277 When a predator comes too close to a killdeer's nest, it flops around pretending to have a broken wing while leading the danger away.

278 The black swallowtail butterfly repels its enemies by sticking out a forked gland—which looks like a snake's tongue—from a pocket behind its head and releasing a foul smell.

279 Thousands of fire ants cling to each other to build a living raft when floods threaten. The queen and larvae are placed in the centre of the raft to ensure the colony's best survival.

DISGUISES

280 To fool predators, a mimic octopus can change its appearance to look like a giant crab, jellyfish, lionfish, mantis shrimp, banded sole, stingray, banded sea krait, or seahorse.

281 A mother cuttlefish camouflages her eggs by placing each one in a capsule, then injecting the capsule with dark ink so as to blend in with the surrounding environment.

DISGUISES

282 The African double-banded courser (bird) lays her eggs next to antelope poop. The eggs have the same colour and pattern as the poop, fooling egg-eating predators.

283 The orchid mantis of Malaysia fools both its prey (mainly insects) and its predators because it looks like a beautiful flower.

284 The leaf-tailed gecko is brown or green and easily blends into tree bark or moss. Its name comes from its flat tail, which looks like a leaf.

285 A masked hunter nymph disguises itself with dust, lint, and other debris so that it can ambush prey such as carpet beetles and bedbugs.

DISGUISES

286 The crested bellbird, native to Australia, fools predators with its ability—like a ventriloquist—to make its voice sound like it is coming from somewhere else than where it is.

287 The caterpillar of the giant swallowtail butterfly looks like a bird dropping to protect it from predators.

288 The decorator crab attaches materials scavenged from its surroundings—such as coral, sponge, seaweed, or anemones—to its shell with tiny hooks that work like Velcro.

289 The goldenrod crab spider can change colour to match the white or yellow flower it is on as it waits to ambush prey.

DISGUISES

290 The wavy-lined emerald caterpillar camouflages itself by attaching flower petals and other plant parts onto its back with silk. When the petals wither, the caterpillar tosses them and puts on a new disguise.

291 Britain's peppered moth has changed its camouflage over time. Initially white with small black specks so as to blend in with light-coloured trees, it gradually darkened to match the tree bark that had darkened with pollution. Now that there is less pollution in Britain, the peppered moth is turning white again.

DEADLY!

292 When the pistol shrimp's claws snap shut it creates a shock wave powerful enough to stun or kill its prey.

293 The golden poison frog is so toxic that touching its skin can kill a human.

294 The net-casting spider captures its prey by tossing a silk net over it.

DEADLY!

295 The archerfish turns its mouth into a water pistol by pressing its tongue against a groove in the roof of its mouth. This forms a tube that can shoot out a jet of water to take down insects in the air or on overhanging vegetation. Amazingly, the archerfish is able to account for the refractive properties of water so as to hit its target exactly.

296 The alligator snapping turtle lies at the bottom of a swamp with its mouth open and its pink, worm-like tongue wriggling to attract passing fish. When a fish comes close enough to take the bait, the turtle snaps its mouth shut.

DEADLY!

297 The assassin bug grabs its prey, stabs it with its sharp proboscis (tubular mouthpart), and fills its prey with toxic saliva. The saliva liquefies the insides of its victim, which the bug then sucks out.

298 The marbled electric ray ambushes a fish, wraps itself around it, and stuns or kills it with an electric shock (up to 200 V) using its electric organs.

299 The bolas spider gives off a chemical that smells like a female moth. When an interested male moth gets close, the spider casts out a sticky silk thread like a fishing line and reels him in.

DEADLY!

300 The bombardier beetle's abdomen has two separate chambers containing chemicals. The two chemicals mix when the beetle senses danger, creating a hot poison that shoots out from its rear end.

301 The trap-door spider lives in a burrow that has a trap door made from silk and soil. When an insect comes close, the door flips open and the spider leaps out, captures its prey, and drags it back to its burrow.

302 The stoat does a strange, hypnotic dance as it slowly approaches its prey. When it gets close enough, it suddenly bites its prey's neck, often killing it instantly.

DEADLY!

303 Japanese honeybees defend themselves from the Asian giant hornet by forming a living ball around it. As the muscles of the bees vibrate, intense heat is generated (up to 47°C; 117°F) which cooks the hornet.

304 The female ant-decapitating fly deposits an egg inside a fire ant. After the egg grows and hatches, the maggot makes its way to the ant's head, where it feeds on its brain, eventually causing the ant's head to fall off.

305 The Australian funnel web spider's venom can be lethal to humans but has no effect on cats and dogs.

TINY TREASURES

306 The world's smallest antelope is the royal antelope. At only 25 cm (10 in) tall, its legs are as thin as chopsticks and its four hooves can fit in a tablespoon.

307 The tardigrade, about 0.5 mm (0.02 in) long, is tough enough to survive boiling water, frozen ice, high doses of radiation, long periods of drought, and being launched into space. If it is in poor health or cannot find a mate, it can produce a clone of itself.

TINY TREASURES

308 The smallest full-grown dog ever known was a Yorkshire terrier named Sylvia that measured 7.5 cm (3 in) tall at the shoulder and weighed only 113 g (4 oz).

309 The Tinkerbell wasp is only 0.25 mm (.01 in) in size.

310 The smallest horse in the world is Thumbelina, a dwarf miniature horse 43 cm (17 in) tall and weighing 26 kg (57 lbs).

311 The bee hummingbird's egg weighs 0.2 g (0.007 oz) and is about the size of a pea.

HUMONGOUS!

312 The Japanese spider crab measures 5.5 m (18 ft) from claw to claw.

313 The barrel sponge is so large (1.8 m; 6 ft) that an average-sized teen could easily fit into it.

314 The ocean sunfish can weigh up to 2200 kg (5000 lbs), about as heavy as a rhinoceros.

HUMONGOUS!

315 The Titan beetle, which measures 16.7 cm (6.6 in), has jaws that are so powerful it can easily snap a pencil in two.

316 The largest bald eagle nest ever recorded was almost 3 m (9.5 ft) in diameter, over 6 m (20 ft) deep and weighed 2.7 tonnes (3 tons).

317 Some of the blood vessels of a blue whale are so large a human can swim through them.

318 The largest salamander in the world is the Chinese giant salamander, which can be up to 1.8 m (6 ft) long.

HUMONGOUS!

319 The Japanese Onagadori, a breed of chicken, have tail feathers that grow up to 8.5 m (28 ft) long.

320 The largest known walking stick, found in Borneo, was 53 cm (21 in) long with its legs stretched out.

321 The tongue of a blue whale weighs over 2700 kg (6000 lbs), about as heavy as an Asian elephant.

322 The world's largest snake is the Amazonian anaconda, which can grow over 9 m (30 ft) long.

OLYMPIC WORTHY

323 The sifaka (lemur) can jump over 9 m (30 ft) as it moves from tree to tree.

324 A flying fish flips its tail up and down about 50 times a second to rise out of the water. Once in the air, it can reach a speed of more than 50 km/h (31 mph).

325 The fastest bird is the peregrine falcon, which can reach speeds of 390 km/h (240 mph) while diving after prey.

OLYMPIC WORTHY

326 A flea can jump 200 times its own body length.

327 The sailfish can swim at a speed of 110 km/h (68 mph).

328 The dung beetle can pull a weight 1141 times heavier than its own body.

329 The cheetah can accelerate from 0 to 97 km/h (60 mph) in three seconds; that's faster than many sports cars.

330 The Asian weaver ant can hold an object that is 100 times its weight—while hanging upside down.

WHEN IT'S COLD OUT

331 About half of the Eastern wood frog's body turns to ice in the winter. First, its eyeballs freeze. Then the frog stops breathing. Then the heart stops beating. When spring comes, the frog thaws out and carries on as usual.

332 During cold weather, Inca doves huddle together in a pyramid formation several tiers high (like cheerleaders). Every few minutes, they rotate positions to ensure all stay warm.

WHEN IT'S COLD OUT

333 The snow leopard keeps warm by wrapping its tail around itself like a blanket.

334 The Antarctic icefish produces antifreeze proteins that prevent its blood from freezing in the cold waters of the Antarctic Ocean.

335 Atlas day geckos, which make their home on snowy mountain peaks, cuddle together to stay warm.

ODDS AND ENDS

The end is near!

336 So as not to lose stability while flying, a bald eagle will drop a feather from one wing if it loses one from the other.

337 Male strawberry poison dart frogs, found in Central American forests, wrestle each other when one tries to go into another's territory. Standing on their back legs, they try to pin each other with their front legs. Once a frog is pinned, the winner—usually the one that lives in that territory—lets it go.

ODDS AND ENDS

338 Crested auklets (seabirds) smell like ripe tangerines.

339 The oldest existing giant barrel sponge is believed to be over 2300 years old.

340 Black lemurs bite millipedes and roll the goo oozing out across their skin to deter parasites and mosquitoes. The glazed eyes and drooling of the lemurs suggests that the goo also acts like a drug.

341 The glass catfish, found in Asian tropical rivers, is virtually invisible because of its transparent skin and muscles. When it dies, the catfish turns milky white.

ODDS AND ENDS

342 Birds don't sweat. To cool down, some birds pant like a dog.

343 The goats of Tamri village in Morocco climb up Argania trees to eat the fruit. The goats can't digest the nut at the centre of the fruit, so it comes out in their poop. Locals collect the droppings, remove the nuts, and crack them open to get at the seeds inside. The seeds are ground and pressed to make expensive Argan oil, used for salad dressings and in cosmetic treatments.

344 Mosquitoes hate catnip but love smelly feet.

345 Every zebra's stripe pattern is unique.

ODDS AND ENDS

346 If you put every insect in the world together on a scale, they would weigh more than all other animals combined.

347 Although polar bears look white, their skin is black and their outer layer of fur is transparent.

348 Piranhas bark like dogs.

349 A bullet ant grows as large as 30 mm (1.2 in) and delivers a sting so powerful it feels like you've been hit with a bullet.

ODDS AND ENDS

350 Pigs are better at playing video games than chimpanzees.

351 There are 40,000 muscles and tendons in an elephant's trunk.

352 Giant tubeworms thrive on the chemical that is released from deep-sea hydrothermal vents although it is deadly to most living things.

353 The venom from ant bites and bee stings have been used to power fuel cells that recharge cell phones, digital cameras, and other electronic devices.

ODDS AND ENDS

354 One tablespoon (10 g) of house dust contains up to 5000 dust mites.

355 There are almost 160 different species of chameleons, ranging from small enough to sit on your finger tip (2.3 cm; 0.9 in) to as big as a cat (69 cm; 27 in).

356 The beaches of Vaadhoo Island in the Indian Ocean turn electric blue at night when bioluminescent phytoplankton called dinoflagellates wash up on shore.

357 Marsh rabbits are both good swimmers and good divers.

ODDS AND ENDS

358 Railroad worms are the only glowworms that produce red light as well as green.

359 Some species of sea urchins cover up with bits of coral and algae to protect themselves from the sun.

360 Opossums are immune to rattlesnake venom.

361 The ribbon eel starts out life as a male that is black with a yellow dorsal fin. As it matures, it turns bright blue with a yellow mouth area. Once it reaches about 1.4 m (4.6 ft) in length, it turns completely yellow and becomes an egg-laying female.

ODDS AND ENDS

362 Females of a newly discovered species of katydid in northern Borneo look exactly like pink leaves.

363 When male chameleons see themselves in a mirror, they think they are seeing a rival and respond by changing to a bright colour to warn it away.

364 Cardinals, butterflies, and lobsters can be female on one side of the body and male on the other side.

365 Without spiders, crop-eating insects would overcome the world, and humans would face famine.

See how many you can answer off the top of your head! Answers are on the page 123.

1. Why do some snails travel in the slime tracks of other snails?

2. What creature has teeth that look almost exactly like human teeth?

3. Which winged creature builds its nest from its own saliva?

4. When trying to impress a potential mate, what does the male satin bowerbird hold in its beak, and why?

5. What does the wrinkle-faced bat do when it's ready to nap?

6. What reptile never closes its eyes?

7. What fish has taste buds all over its body?

8. What does otter poop smell like?

9. What are the three things a horny toad might do to deter a predator?

10. Which bird is a good ventriloquist?

11. Which creature's venom can be deadly to humans but has no effect on cats and dogs?

12. What body part of the blue whale is as heavy as an elephant?

13. Which mountain dwellers cuddle to stay warm?

14. What do black lemurs do with millipedes, and why?

15. Why do some island beaches in the Indian Ocean glow electric blue at night?

1. To save energy (#14).
2. Pacu fish (#25).
3. Cave-dwelling swiftlet (#46).
4. Something blue to highlight his colouring (#90).
5. Pulls up a flap of skin over its face (#164).
6. A snake (#185).
7. A catfish (#221).
8. Jasmine tea (#231).
9. Flattens itself on the ground, puffs up its body, squirts blood from its eye (#264).
10. Crested bellbird (#286).
11. Funnel web spider (#305).
12. Its tongue (#321).
13. Atlas day geckos (#335).
14. They bite the millipede and rub the goo on their skin to deter parasites and mosquitoes (#340).
15. Bioluminescent phytoplankton wash up on their shore (#356).

AUTHOR'S NOTE

The information contained in this book was researched and verified with the most accurate resources available. Sources included newspapers, magazines, books, documentaries, and websites. However, the field of science is ever changing, and what may be accepted as fact today may be discarded tomorrow as new knowledge surfaces. I have done my very best to bring you the most interesting and accurate tidbits of information I can at the time of publication.

If you are a writer, artist, or aspiring creative, our companion book *When Sleeping Birds Fly for the Creative Soul* will motivate you to bring your creativity to an entirely new level. You might just get inspiration for your next story, poem, or artwork!

Sally Meadows is an award-winning author, recording artist, and speaker from Saskatchewan, Canada. A former scientist, children's entertainer, and educator, Sally is passionate about sharing amazing science facts with curious readers of all ages. This is her third book.

You can connect with Sally
at https://sallymeadows.com,
at sally@sallymeadows.com,
at https://www.facebook.com/SallyMeadowsMusic,
at https://instagram.com/sallymeadowsmusic,
and on Twitter @SallyMeadows.

ALSO BY THE AUTHOR

The Two Trees

Beneath That Star

The Underdog Duckling

COMING SOON!

*When Sleeping Birds Fly
For The Creative Soul*

*When Crocodiles Cry:
365 More Amazing Facts About
The Animal Kingdom*

*When Jellyfish Rain From The Sky:
365 Amazing Facts About
The World Around Us*

To keep up with all her news,
sign up for Sally's newsletter at
https://sallymeadows.com.

www.ingramcontent.com/pod-product-compliance
Lightning Source LLC
Chambersburg PA
CBHW030528080526
44586CB00011B/356